T0106289

Dancing Naked Before God

Fitzroy Othello Jr.

WestBow
PRESS
A DIVISION OF THOMAS NELSON

WestBow Press books may be ordered through booksellers or by contacting:

WestBow Press
A Division of Thomas Nelson
1663 Liberty Drive
Bloomington, IN 47403
www.westbowpress.com
1-(866) 928-1240

Because of the dynamic nature of the Internet, any web addresses or links contained in this book may have changed since publication and may no longer be valid. The views expressed in this work are solely those of the author and do not necessarily reflect the views of the publisher, and the publisher hereby disclaims any responsibility for them.

Any people depicted in stock imagery provided by Thinkstock are models, and such images are being used for illustrative purposes only.

Certain stock imagery © Thinkstock.

ISBN: 978-1-4497-3253-0 (sc)
ISBN: 978-1-4497-3252-3 (e)

Library of Congress Control Number: 2011961167

Printed in the United States of America

WestBow Press rev. date: 12/06/2011

WARNING!

It is not normal to open a book with a warning, but as you will discover, this is no normal book. This book is meant to destroy your paradigms about God and His creation and give you a radically new one. It is meant, therefore, to change the world one life at a time and one reader at a time.

So first let me begin with an apology on behalf of the church of Jesus Christ. I apologize to you on behalf of the church for the terrible condition the world is in today and for the great trauma that will soon come upon it and has already begun. We have failed at almost every turn to be salt and light to the earth; therefore, you shall hate us and persecute us (Matthew 5:13–16).

The result of our failure is that the earth is now in crisis and darkness, while we continue, for the most part, to indulge in religion and cultism that is even now embracing mysticism. You will therefore be used by God to judge and thereby purify His church in the earth (Malachi 3:1–3, Daniel 7:21, Matthew 24:9–12).

This is because Christianity was never meant to be a religion but a dynamic, intimate relationship between God and man through His Son, Jesus Christ, based upon the type of extravagant love that David displayed for God when he danced naked before Him (2 Samuel 6:14–23).

At several stages in history, Satan and then man rejected such a relationship with God the Father, in favor of religion and rebellion, and drastic action has always been taken by the Father to turn His creation back to Himself.

This is because man has a basic problem with the terms that God has laid down for this relationship, which are man's absolute surrender to the lordship of God and subsequent obedience to His perfect will. This is only possible if man loves God with the wanton abandon shown by David (Deuteronomy 6:5, Matthew 37–40).

Mankind's problem with God's terms and conditions for relationship with Himself, however, is not unique. Satan had the same problem. He was the first being to grow tired of complete submission to God and instead devised His own plan of action based upon this decision:

"I will exalt my throne above the stars of God; I will sit upon the assembly of the uttermost north. I will ascend above the heights of the clouds; I will make myself like the Most High"(Isaiah 14:13–14).

The basis of this decision was pride. He decided that God, who created him, had no right to define his existence. Therefore, he would reject God's order and establish a new paradigm for himself, the angels who would follow him, and ultimately God's greatest creation, mankind itself. He found God's way to be restrictive to his personal desires for self-definition, so he began rebellion in creation.

The cost to him was terrible:

"How you have fallen from heaven, O light-bringer and daystar, son of the morning! How you have been cut down to the ground, you who weakened and laid low the nations" (Isaiah 14:12).

He was transformed from the most glorious created being, Lucifer, into the fallen Satan. He is now the grotesque ruler over the pit, or hell, where he is lord over the angels who fell with him and the souls of rebellious men, whom he torments. Lucifer had precious stones, such as diamonds, and musical instruments built into him. He was the praise and worship leader in heaven and ruled over the earth, positioned between God and creation in worship until he became proud in his heart (Ezekiel 28:13–19).

This book explores, among other things, how Satan has convinced man to be a fallen being like himself by man's rejection of absolute submission to the will of God and how God has therefore used Satan to sift mankind of rebels to His design for creation, until only those who love Him enough to submit to Him remain in eternal joy.

"For behold, I create new heavens and a new earth. And the former things shall not be remembered or come into mind. But be glad and rejoice forever in that which I create; for behold, I create Jerusalem to be a rejoicing and her people a joy. And I will rejoice in Jerusalem and be glad in my people; and the sounds of weeping will no more be heard in it, or the cry of distress" (Isaiah 65:17–19).

Then I saw a new sky (heaven) and a new earth, for the former sky and the former earth had passed away (vanished), and there no longer existed any sea. And I saw the holy city, the new Jerusalem, descending out of heaven from God, all arrayed like a bride beautified and adorned for her husband. Then I heard a mighty voice from the throne and I perceived its distinct words, saying, "See! The abode of God is with men; He will live (encamp, tent) among them, and God shall personally be with them and be their God. God will wipe away every tear from their eyes, and death shall be no more; neither shall there be any anguish (sorrow and mourning) nor grief nor pain anymore, for the old conditions and the former order of things have passed away.

However, those who reject God's order through pride shall along with he who was their progenitor in pride (Satan) be thrown into the lake of fire where they shall burn forever (Revelation 20:10, 15). The supreme irony of this tragedy is that they will discover that even before the foundations of the earth were laid, God the Father knew their choice and that they would be forgotten by all of creation as though they never existed (Ephesians 2:10). What will you choose?

Contents

Chapter 1

Let the Praise Begin!

"Then from the throne there came a voice, saying, Praise our God, all you servants of His, you who reverence Him, both small and great!" (Revelation 19:5)

A bride is being prepared in the earth for her lover and her Lord, and the time of His coming is so close that I can feel it in my bones. The feel of it makes me sing on my bed at night, for my eyes have seen the King of Eternity, the Lamb upon the throne Who reigns forever. He has overcome rebellion against God and its terrible effects upon creation by living a sinless life and dying as the Lamb of God and being raised on the third day as the conquering Lion of the tribe of Judah. Then He ascended to sit next to the Father on His throne as the King of all Kings and the Lord of all Lords.

Several years ago, I became aware of the fact that Christ is coming sooner than most of us believe. I cannot give a time period, but I know that His coming is soon. This was quite a revelation to me, because at the time it came to me, my credo was "work hard, play harder"—and my play was not biblically approved, to say the least. At that time, I was a student at the University of the West Indies (UWI) on the island of Trinidad in the Caribbean, reading for a degree in English.

Play, to me, was riotous living, and work was my effort to graduate with honors. This island is my home and has been for all of my life, so quite naturally, I knew where all the best spots to play were. In other words, the nightclubs and pubs. I was not always inclined to find my entertainment in this manner. I grew up as a pastor's kid in a Baptist denomination on my island.

However, during my early teens, I began to have unusual difficulties coping with life. In addition to the "normal teenage traumas" of newfound sexuality, alcohol, and peer pressure, I was faced with the dilemma of having been born a seer. From birth, I have been a prophet like Jeremiah (Jeremiah 1:5), with the ability to see into the supernatural and possessed of great spiritual insight and abilities.

I have always enjoyed a very close walk with the Holy Spirit, and as a young child, He told me to tell no one of my spiritual inclination. So I kept silent and led a secret life as a seer for most of my life until my secret life and my public life collided, leaving my life a twisted heap of wreckage when I was diagnosed as schizophrenic by a psychiatrist whose paradigm of life had no room for my existence as a perfectly sane individual.

At five years old, I had the first visitation that I can remember by the Father. I was in my bedroom, sitting at my table, when the spiritual atmosphere of the room suddenly changed. There was a huge, golden beam of light in front of me, and God spoke to me out of the midst of it.

He showed me what He wanted my future to be and asked me if I would accept it. Enraptured by His presence, in which I felt only raw, unlimited love, authority, and power, I agreed to His proposal for my future. However, after He left, time and a different reality seemed to resume. Time seems to stop in His presence. I was shocked and heartbroken. All I have ever truly wanted from that moment is to return to that level of His presence.

To make matters worse, I was instructed by Him to tell nobody of this encounter, and I could remember none of what I was told my future would be. For the first time, having grown up in a deeply loving and nurturing family made up of my parents and three older sisters, I felt truly alone in the world and cried out to the Father to return.

He did not do so at first, but the presence of the Holy Spirit in and around me radically increased, along with my spiritual abilities and insight. I would later have further visits from the Father and Jesus Himself, with the Holy Spirit always being with me as my close friend and advisor.

Satan immediately began to woo me. I would wake up 5:00 a.m. on a regular basis, hearing the faint sound of an African drummer on his instrument calling to me. It was the call of the religious heritage chosen by many Africans, and it was a very powerful call, especially for one as young as I was and also seeking spiritual belonging. I knew in my heart that all I had to do was reach out with my spirit and a connection would be made with this drummer and all behind him, spiritually and physically.

Thank God I had a grandmother who was herself a deeply spiritual person and who was very devoted to prayer. She was my personal intercessor, and until she died six years later, she remained my spiritual lifeline and covered my life in prayer and fasting. My parents told me that she was powerfully drawn to me as a child and took to me as though I was her own child. I believe to this day that if it had not been for the protective covering of my relationship with her, I would have answered that call from that nameless, faceless drummer, thus forever altering my destiny.

One of the most important things that my parents did for me when I was a child was to give me a book of Bible stories containing some of the most beautiful pictures I have ever seen. The Holy Spirit then began to teach me how to think visually through strong mental and spiritual images or visions, and I do so to this day. That book also firmly established in my young soul that my heritage was Judeo-Christian in nature.

3

This is all of my childhood that I have been allowed to share with you in this book to this point. I can also say that I do not know when the drumming stopped, yet even to this day, the drums of Africa still call to my soul.

At thirteen years old, I was allowed by God to decide that I could no longer handle the situations that serving Him manifested in my life. I then drifted further and further away from Him until I entered university at age twenty-one. My past then caught up with me. Satan was no longer satisfied with me being a backslidden believer and told me that I had no choice but to serve him or else.

You see, for me, there has never been the possibility of being religious. My spiritual sensitivity has always meant that I would eventually be either the bondslave of Christ or the slave of Satan. There was never any middle ground for me. Trust me— I definitely tried to find it! It could not even exist in my mind alone as a delusion, as it is with most people in the world. You either serve God or Satan; there is no demilitarized zone. Reality is a perfect dichotomy.

At the end of my first semester in university, I got into a terrible accident, and I realized that a warlock was behind it. To put it mildly, I got very angry. By this time, I'd had a few encounters with sorcerers, and I had won each relatively easily, considering what was to follow. I knew that I needed help, so as usual, I selectively told my parents what had taken place.

We got together in the room in our house where we gather to pray and took authority over the situation in the supernatural realms. Yes, some Baptists know how to do this. However, this was no usual spiritual conflict. It was to spill over into and dominate my life in the natural realm as well and would last for sixteen years. This was the climax of a period of my life that began at the death of my paternal grandmother, as the Lord had renewed His covenant with me a few months after she died.

Almost immediately, Satan approached me in a dream, pretending to be my grandmother, knowing how lost I now felt without her.

However, the Holy Spirit warned me that it was Satan and woke me up. Since then, it has been a straight, no-holds-barred battle between God and Satan for my soul.

When I was thirteen years old, Satan visited me, and during a conversation with me that the Father allowed, Satan told me that if I served him, his people would worship me as a god. He said that the dark color of my skin would not be an issue, but if I continued in my walk with God, I would be called a madman by the church of Jesus Christ and would be institutionalized as a result of this.

Alarmingly enough, this threat did come to pass many years later! However, that's another story for another time.

Chapter 2

The Purpose Of Christ

When we see Him, we shall be like Him …

The terrible tragedy of the church of Jesus Christ today is that some two thousand years after His death, most of us do not fully know why He came to the earth. If we did, the world would be a garden of delight—the planting of the Lord.

How can I make such a bold statement? Simple: I always humble myself absolutely before the Lord in the manner of the saints who have gone before. I use the grace of God that we all have to go boldly before the throne of God in the name of His Son, Jesus Christ, and ask Him, *"WHY, DADDY?"*

This is no small thing! Several years ago, after reading the Bible and looking at the church of Jesus Christ, I realized that the church was not working. I saw Satan making tremendous gains on seemingly every side and the church retreating into a falsely protective shell behind its own walls. I was tremendously disturbed by this and asked God to show me how I could make a difference for Him.

I cannot remember when or how, but He began to respond to my question and offer of remedial service. I believe that He spoke into my spirit by impression that the church today is in the same state that Israel was in during the time of Christ: we do not know Him as the Father of our faith that Abraham did.

"You do not know where I am coming from or where I am going" (Isaiah 8:14).

Abraham knew God so intimately that he was able to physically identify Him when God visited him. He was also personally informed by the Father of what He was going to do on His way to destroy Sodom before He did it, as a sign of His respect for Abraham! Do we today as a church accurately know what the Father is doing and is about to do, or are we as confused as the world and turning to the world for directions? As you may have guessed, this is a purely rhetorical question.

Instead, we do as the church of Jesus' day, Israel, did and set ourselves up to judge according to the flesh (by what we see and hear). We condemn by external, human standards, whereas Christ Himself does not judge or condemn or sentence anyone (Isaiah 8:15).

Yet even when He does judge, His judgment is true and His decision is right, because He is not alone in making it but makes it with the Father. For according to the law, the testimony or evidence of two persons is reliable and valid (Deuteronomy 19:15). So He said to the Pharisees:

"If you were (truly) Abraham's children, then you would do the works of Abraham (follow his example, do as Abraham did)" v.39.

God's purpose for creating man was to recreate beings just like Him to be His intimate friends forever. This is why He created man in His own image and likeness and gave to us complete authority over His creation (Genesis 1:26–29). However, man at first was from the earth into which God blew the breath of life.

He always intended to go beyond this. That is why Christ is the Lamb that was slain even before the foundations of the earth were laid. Christ, the second person of the Trinity and therefore the physical manifestation of God Himself, is the Last or Final Adam.

What does this mean? The answer to this is the mystery of God and Christ spoken of by the apostle Paul.

God always intended for man to be in his final state totally from above or of heaven and not of the earth below, even while living on the earth. So the first Adam was of the earth, but Christ, the Last Adam, is from above. True Christians are not of the first Adam but the Final.

This is why when Enoch, the seventh son of a seventh son—with seven being the biblical number for completion—became so much like the Father because of his intimacy with Him, God had no choice but to rapture him as an example to us of his precondition for us to be so taken up to heaven. He was not and yet he was, until he no longer could dwell with man (Genesis 5:22–24).

"And all of us, as with unveiled face, (because we) continued to behold (in the Word of God) as in a mirror the glory of the Lord, are constantly being transfigured into His very own image in ever increasing splendor and from one degree of glory to another; (for this comes) from the Lord (Who is) the Spirit" (2 Corinthians 3:18).

Enoch grew to be so much like God through constantly walking with Him because that was his *only* purpose for being on the earth. He was to give God pleasure, thereby progressively becoming just like God; when this process was completed, God took Him out of the earth realm to be with Himself forever. Since the visitation from God that I experienced as a child, this has been both my dream and my life's only quest.

I have been led astray by my own physical desires at times, but this level of union with God has always been my goal. This was so even before I had the theology to support it and just desired it in my heart. You see, once you enter the physically tangible presence of God, you shall surely be spoiled for life. It is something you never forget.

Access to this level of the presence of God has been a rare thing throughout human history. Yet it is what I live and die for each day as I lay down my own desires as a sacrifice to do what pleases

God. To be able to do this effectively, I had to first discover that it is humanly impossible to do so.

This discovery was the result of a process that began on New Year's Eve 1994 in the collision between my secret life and my public life. I was in a relative's van on my way to the night watch church service, and I had also packed to return to my residence at the university.

My mind was not on church but on two trysts I had set up with two beautiful young women. You may wonder why I'm including these details. It is because I refuse to write and not be real; otherwise my writing is useless and purely the function of pride, succumbing to which is my greatest concern in life.

In the vehicle was my relative, his friend, and me. As we turned a corner, God opened up the spiritual realm to me, and I saw three very powerful spirits working against me in the heavens. This was not the first time this had happened. Four years before, precisely the same thing had happened to me, with similar results.

I was at home in the south of the island and received an invitation to a bachelor party in the north. My father told me not to go, because there was a state of emergency in effect on the island after an attempted revolution. There was an eight o'clock curfew. Hothead that I was, I went anyway.

Later that night, while turning into a street on the way to the party, God opened up the spiritual world to me and showed me the same spirits acting against me. I then felt a tremendous urge to tell the driver of the car to stop immediately. Afraid of being considered a nut for doing such a thing in the presence of these three grown men I was hanging out with, I remained silent.

At the end of the street, we found ourselves in a police roadblock, at which we were arrested for breaking curfew. We spent that night in a dirty, foul-smelling jail cell. A pretty police officer felt sorry for me and gave me several sheets of newspaper to spread on the floor to sleep. My companions invited themselves to a share of this covering for the cold, hard, dirty floor.

The police officer made my night in jail bearable by talking with me. The next morning, a relative who was a judge got us out of jail. Needless to say, the genius that I was I learned precious little from that experience.

The next time around, for months I found myself repeatedly dreaming of being badly hurt in a car accident. The accident in the dream was very similar to one a relative had told me he was once involved in, so I thought it was just a developing phobia. The result was that years later, I again entered a street and did nothing when warned of danger by God.

As we turned a corner, with loud calypso music playing on the radio, we were hit head on by a speeding car driven by a drunk. As it became obvious that this was going to hurt a whole lot, I began to think I was dreaming again. Time seemed to slow down while in a blur of futile activity, my relative pulled the van hard left.

I remember being pitched forward at tremendous speed and crashing into the van's dashboard and the steering wheel. In a daze, I just wanted to get out of the vehicle—as though that would make everything better, or better yet, that I would wake up.

Covered in my own blood in my favorite party shirt, I could only cry out to God, asking Him, "Why?"

The cold, silent night was my only response, so I changed my plea to one for mercy. I could also hear my relative somewhere nearby in the darkness, also repeatedly crying out, "Lord, have mercy!"

When I tried to open my eyes, I discovered that they were filled with glass from the shattered windshield. The doctors at the hospital later washed as much of the glass out of my eyes as they could, but to my horror, I was told that there was glass *inside* my eyes. These pieces of glass were too close to my retina for them to be surgically removed.

The ophthalmologist at the hospital later told me that I had to hope that my eyes would reject the pieces of glass as foreign objects, thereby pushing them out. The look on his face said that he did not really believe this would happen.

I was in a really bad way. My face and head were badly scarred, and I had the glass in my eyes. In my distress, I chose to return to the faith of my grandmother. I began to pray again. I really got into the face of God, asking His forgiveness for my lifestyle and for healing.

He answered. Several weeks after the accident, I was alone in my room when I felt His presence. "You were wrestling with me," is all I can remember Him saying to me during that conversation. I vowed to change my way of living, and He left.

A month later, I was sleeping over at a relative's home, and I felt God's presence upon me. "Go to the sink," I heard His voice say. When I got to the sink, I felt the Holy Spirit moving upon my right eyeball, and the pieces of glass in it fell into the sink.

In a similar experience several days later, God removed all the glass from my left eye. I will never forget the look of shock on the doctor's face when I told him what had happened and he could find no trace of glass in either of my eyes. Next the scars on my face and head "settled." One of these was an ugly, two-inch-long gash beneath my lips, where I had been cut through to my mouth. I had broken down sobbing the first time I saw it, thinking that I would look as though I had three lips for the rest of my life. By the grace of God, it would now take a close examination to detect these scars.

Chapter 3

Dancing Naked Before God

"And David danced before the Lord with all his might, clad in a linen ephod (a priest's upper garment) … Then David returned to bless his household. And (his wife) Michal daughter of Saul came out to meet David and said, how glorious was the king of Israel today, who stripped himself of his kingly robes and uncovered himself in the eyes of his servants' maids as one of the worthless fellows shamelessly uncovers himself!" (2 Samuel 6:14, 20)

It is impossible to truly please God without dancing naked before Him. He demands this of those who would draw close to Him. Now, don't go taking your clothes off! At least not yet. This requirement is most often a symbolic gesture in which you declare yourself as His property in a way that means that you reject conventional human wisdom and the status quo. An example of this is receiving water baptism.

In the process of biblical adult water baptism, the individual changes his conventional way of behaving. In many cases, he is led into the water by another person, instead of choosing his own course. When he is in the deep, he is then unexpectedly plunged backward, not forward into often cold water and brought back to the surface, gasping for air, only when the immerser or baptizer sees fit to bring him up.

I can only imagine the fun some baptizers must have when they get together for drinks after this powerful ritual. (Just kidding!)

Baptizer 1: "You should have seen the look on his face when I hesitated before bringing him back up."

Baptizer 2: (Laughing out loud) "He looked like he thought we were going to drown him."

Baptizer 1: "Because of the kind of sin he was in before he got saved, I was tempted to leave him down longer!"

Baptizer 2: (Chuckles to himself) "There was real fear in the poor guy's eyes."

Baptizer 1: Do you think anyone would believe that this is how we get our entertainment?

Baptizer 2: "Nah!" (Both laughing)

On a more serious note, it is important to point out that the spiritual man is not consciously led into any situation knowing much about it. However, a Christian who is carnal is responsible in the eyes of society and believes that he chooses his own path in life with care. This is human wisdom. In the Spirit, we are led into a new life, reality, and kingdom when we accept Jesus Christ as Lord and Savior. After this, we are baptized with the Holy Spirit and with fire from heaven.

This powerful person from heaven then takes control of the life of the individual who has surrendered himself to him and leads him into the deep things of the Spirit. He then submerges such a person in the supernatural and takes total control of his interface between the spiritual and the physical worlds.

Let us be real! This can often make us very afraid. If we truly let the Holy Spirit reign in our lives, He takes control of our very grip on all reality, both physical and spiritual.

Our sanity itself can therefore seem to be at risk when we enter into the really deep things of God. This is the realm in which Jesus Christ, our example, walked following in the footsteps of David and Abraham! These are the fathers of our faith, to the extent that God calls Jesus Christ His servant David and the son of David.

So when we speak of the faith of our fathers, this is what we are speaking of. We must therefore always be in the state of dancing naked before God. We will find this impossible without childlike trust in God. This is why Jesus told the leader of the Jews, Nicodemus, that one must first be born again if he is to enter into the kingdom of heaven. One must therefore become a new and radically different type of individual from the normal, rational man (John 3:1–13).

The born-again experience is not manifested by speaking in tongues. These are not the words of Jesus Christ Who came to earth to open the born-again experience to all men! It is a way of living, thinking, and most essentially *being!* Now is the time for the church to move beyond childish "milk doctrines" that may impress and entertain us but lack true power and authority to transform individuals, institutions, and nations.

Most people who call themselves Christians and "born again" and genuinely believe that they belong to the kingdom of heaven are therefore not what they think. They have chosen to adopt a Western religion that has little to do with the absolute lordship of the Hebrew Messiah in the life of the believer. This belief system is totally opposed to original Judeo-Christianity. However, it does make billions feel good and is thus called a panacea for the masses by the world.

Authentic Judeo-Christianity begins with and is made up and ends with the absolute rule of Jesus Christ the Messiah in the life of the believer. This is the true basis of our relationship with Him. This is why the apostle Paul who had the most powerful encounter with

Messiah as the risen Lord was chosen to write most of the New Testament.

This lack of understanding is destroying much of the church. Most of today's believers say crazy things like "This is who I am, and I have no intention of changing, not even to become like the Last Adam, Jesus Christ." They delude themselves with the new doctrine that God loves them just the way they are and will accept them because of Christ's sacrifice on Calvary. Many are now even ludicrously preaching that we can enter heaven with unrepented sin in our lives!

The belief in sacrifice that was the pillar of Christianity has largely been thrown out of the church that is not at present being persecuted in the earth. Not to mention the belief that great suffering at some point in time is par for the course in the life of the disciple of the Christ. "Many are the afflictions of the righteous, but in the end God delivers them." Then we genuinely ask why the Western church lacks power and authority!

I was bowled over theologically when I first heard a young man read Luke 14:33:

"So then, any of you who does not forsake (renounce, surrender claim to, give up, say good-bye to) all that he has cannot be my disciple."

The implications of this Scripture are simply staggering! This is the first condition for becoming a disciple of Christ, as stated by Jesus Himself. Have you met it? I certainly did not until I was twenty-two years old. In a moment of meditation on the word and rare intimacy with the Spirit of Christ, I cried out Him.

"Lord, take my life and do whatever You want to do with it. All I truly want is all of Your presence always. Break down whatever you want to break down. Build whatever you want to build. I just want You to always be with me!"

I had no idea what I was getting myself into, but I meant it with all my heart. In His presence, I found perfect joy and eternal treasures that I cannot begin to describe. My life also immediately began to come apart.

A few days later, as I sat in a history tutorial, I saw a powerful evil spirit leaving a nearby religious area and moving toward me. My first reaction was that God would let it do me no harm, so I ignored it. I did not even pray, because the Spirit did not lead me to do so, and the first lesson in true spiritual warfare is absolute surrender of your will to that of the Holy Spirit. If you do not do this, you will not even be allowed into this theatre of conflict by God, because Satan will steal from you, kill you, and destroy you. For him, it would be like taking candy from a baby!

To my horror, the powerful evil spirit was allowed to come against my mind. To say that this was not a pleasant experience for a seer such as me is a gross understatement. I saw it, felt it, and lived it! These attacks continued for three weeks, during which time I began to hallucinate terribly. I was also negatively affected in other ways that I cannot mention.

This was not what I had expected when I made my heartfelt declaration to the Lord to take over my life. Yet here it was, taking place. I now had to depend on the Holy Spirit to show me what was real and what was not, as the hallucinations became a feature of my life.

I was now unable to go to classes at the university, and my parents found out. Then evil spirits began to be allowed to come against me at night, and I could rarely sleep. However, God began to give me supernatural energy to take me through the day. When prayer seemed to have failed them, my parents told me that I was being taken to a doctor.

Led to believe it was a normal doctor, I went along. However, I soon found myself seated before a psychiatrist. After she interviewed me, she diagnosed me as schizophrenic. For the second time, God had destroyed my life. I felt completely betrayed by my lover and my Lord.

This was the beginning of the end of my old life. I knew it, and I was in a state of complete shock. I was like Peter when Christ began to preach a then-offensive doctrine of eating His flesh and drinking His blood. I was confused and hurt even worse than when I had to repeat a year at school at thirteen years old, but I could not depart from Jesus Christ again.

The pain had only just begun. I was put on a barbaric medication that wiped me out. All I could do was sleep and eat for several months, as I took a semester off from my studies. My true higher learning was now in full swing. I had to depend on the Holy Spirit to do anything during the short periods of time I spent awake and to protect me from evil when I slept.

Many times, I had to beg my mother to sleep next to me at night. The mental, emotional, and other defenses that God had given me as a child as my grandmother prayed over me were now broken down by chemicals in the medication I was taking. Evil spirits found open doors through which they came to torment me.

I am not talking about science fiction or fantasy. I truly have and need such defenses that are built and controlled by the Holy Spirit. We *all* do!

Even my will to live was under constant assault, as I discovered what depression and oppression truly mean.

Finally I had to go back to school to complete my degree. I could no longer stay near the campus and away from home, so I had to get a ride from a friend who lived near me and was also a student at the university. God gave me the strength and will to wake up and get ready to go to my classes. I would then crash into medicated sleep as soon as I got into his car.

The Holy Spirit would then wake me when I reached the university, and I would find a place to crash again until I had a lecture. He would lead me like a child, telling me which classes to go to and which to sleep through. I was also told which notes to take and which to ignore, and later which questions and topics would come for the final examinations for each course I studied.

Nobody knew the torment I was going through, and when I tried to tell my family, they either ignored me or sent me back to the doctors, who later prescribed more medication. In these circumstances, keeping my mouth shut was a vital discipline that I have learned well. During my years on medication, I came to the brink of true insanity more times than I could count. However, each time the Holy Spirit would painstakingly pull me back.

I lost the will to live for many months, and three times I was on the verge of killing myself, only to be physically stopped by the Holy Spirit. I began to spend long periods praying that God would take my life, because I could stand it no more, and each time I was led by the Spirit to repent. Interestingly, this was also the period of some of my most powerful experiences with God, angels, archangels and angelic beings. I was always conscious of at least one very powerful angel accompanying and advising me in everything concerning myself and others. I entered into experiences and realms and dimensions and levels in the Spirit that I cannot yet begin to describe.

I truly experienced both heaven and hell, tremendous joy and nightmarish pain, all during a period of fifteen years. I have chosen to forget those years because my psyche simply cannot bear the ferocity and ecstasy of their memories. So forgetting the things that are behind me, I continue to dance naked before God, my lover, and my Lord.

Chapter 4

God's Problem with Man

SIN

From the garden of Eden to today's global civilization, God has had a basic problem with man. This is that very few people throughout the millennia of human civilizations have been able to obey Him in the manner that He demands. Anything less is sin.

Man is God's greatest creation and His first creation to be given the power of choice and free will. However, man has not been able to handle this power!

Eve's dilemma in the garden when faced with choice highlights this (Genesis 5:6): "So when the woman saw that the tree was good for food, that it was pleasant to the eyes, and a tree desirable to make one wise, she took of its fruit and ate. She also gave to her husband with her and he ate."

It is critical to this book to see that what God had said to Adam and thus Eve made no sense to them both when presented with the power of choice and self-determination! The Bible does not deny that the food was good for food. Why should Adam and Eve not eat something that was good for food? It was also attractive or pleasant to the eyes. If that was not enough, the Bible says that the tree would be good to make her wise. The rest is history.

Some would argue that the poor suckers did not stand a chance in that scenario. Why obey God and not eat the forbidden fruit, when everything you could see from your own wisdom and experience told you that you would enjoy eating it and that there was nothing very wrong with eating it, from your perspective?

The answer is simply that they should have loved God enough not to! If they had, they would still literally be dancing naked before God in a perfect world to this day. However, from the first, man could not love God the way that He demanded that His greatest creation love Him. This is true, despite the fact that He came down from heaven and walked and talked with Adam in the garden in the cool of the day.

God has faced the same problem with every generation of Adam's descendants, save a few individuals called the elect of God. Abel was one member of the elect. God demanded a sacrifice for the sin of man and the curse that it had brought upon the earth. Abel loved God enough to obey Him.

Cain made the same mistake that his parents did. He was a farmer and so produce was what was most precious to him. Naturally, he thought that God would be pleased if he gave to Him a sacrifice from his best. He genuinely wanted to please God. However, like his parents, he resorted to his own reason and ignored the commandment of God. God's frustration with man could be seen in His response to Cain: "Why could you just not have been obedient like your brother?"

The problem man faces when presented with choice is that his own fallen wisdom tells him that God is wrong! And not just wrong, but unreasonably so. This is because from the very first, God has demanded a radical love from man that defies human reason.

After the fall of man in the garden of Eden, it became not only unreasonable in the eyes of man to obey God, it also became contrary to His very nature.

Proverbs 14:12: "There is a way that seems right to man, But its end is the way of death."

If this was not enough, fallen man then created kingdoms based upon his own fallen wisdom and therefore controlled by God's greatest adversary, Satan. This is why Jesus Christ did not deny that the kingdoms of the world and their glory were Satan's to give to Him if he chose to obey the tempter (Matthew 4:8, 9). However, Jesus loved God the Father enough to obey Him, even when offered the whole world. Most of humanity has disobeyed God for much less than this.

The apostle Paul was therefore forced to admit on behalf of God that fallen man in the form of the tribe of Israel could not love God enough to obey Him and keep His laws. God was always aware of this. Therefore, he was always prepared for this situation. This is why Jesus Christ is the Lamb that was slain, even "before the foundations of the earth were laid." God always has a plan to get His way, although most individuals never love Him enough to obey Him.

That plan is the work of the Holy Spirit, Who was sent to the earth after the crucifixion of Jesus Christ upon our hearts. Jeremiah 31:33b: "I will put my law in their minds and write it on their hearts; and I will be their God, and they shall be my people."

Ezekiel 36:26–28: "I will give you a new heart and put a new spirit within you; I will take the heart of stone out of your flesh and give you a heart of flesh. I will put my Spirit within you and cause you to walk in my statutes, and you will keep my judgments and do them. Then you shall dwell in the land that I gave to your fathers; you shall be my people and I will be your God."

The problem is that the work of the Holy Spirit in us, which is compared to a circumcision and crucifixion, hurts sometimes just as much as both of these experiences, and most of us don't love God enough to choose it! We have therefore chosen to not dance naked before God and be *respectable* to the world.

Chapter 5

Wisdom Builds a House Called Dominion

In ancient times, God's Spirit offered herself to man as the Lady Wisdom or the Spirit of Wisdom. Her purpose was the same then as it is today: to convince man to abandon his fallen wisdom and obey God because he loves Him as only the elect saints do. To such saints He gives dominion in the earth (Proverbs 8:1–7, 9:1–6).

Obedience to God is therefore the thing that God requires most from man. The more ridiculous God's will seems to be or the more impossible or sometimes even painful the price of that obedience is, the more God values it as a sign of our great love for Him. This is why He blessed Abraham and David among others as He did. Abraham was prepared to offer up his precious and only son that He had waited for His whole life, as a sacrifice to God. God had to send an angel to stop him. Can there be any greater example of someone dancing naked before God?

David not only took his clothes off to dance naked before God, but he also made a point of stating that he would not offer up a sacrifice to God unless it cost him something precious. This is not an example of human wisdom or duty, which would only lead us to empty religion, but of a love that is both pure and beautiful. Such a love abandons all human logic in wanton delight in service and worship unto God. This why Abraham is the father of our faith and why God states that He loves a cheerful giver!

God Himself says that such wisdom defies human logic in Proverbs 3:5–7.

This is why God's remnant or elect in the earth are seldom large in number but are great in the eyes of God. He goes as far as to say that the world is not worthy of such saints in His eyes (Hebrews 11:36).

We must thus always seriously consider our ways when others understand us and embrace us as one of their group. The truly spiritual man is understood by no man but discerns all things. Jesus Christ Himself said that if we are His followers, we would be hated by men, for a servant is not greater than his master. If the master is hated, then the servant would be too. Are you hated by men for the gospel's sake? Are you persecuted and despised and abused for your faith? If this has never happened to us, then are we really Christians or Christlike ones in the earth?

The greatest miracle takes place when we love God enough to obey Him despite such a price for our obedience. He draws us into such a close walk with Him that we progressively become more and more like Him. Enoch mastered this level of loving obedience to God so much that he enjoyed the most profound walk recorded in the Bible.

Beloved God grew to love Enoch so much because of his loving and wanton obedience of the Father that He could no longer bear any separation from His beloved son. Therefore He translated Enoch to heaven without him having to die.

Enoch also became so similar to God during his intimate relationship with the Father that He became just like Him. He was totally of God and not of this world or fallen flesh or Satan. A just and loving God therefore had to reward his son by translating him to heaven.

This is why obedience is better than sacrifices such as the sacrifice of praise with our lips! Many of us claim Christ with our lips, but our hearts are far from Him.

Such costly obedience is therefore one of the conditions that each saint must meet to be raptured by God, because there is a divine principle called the Law of First Mention in the Bible. This law holds that when something is mentioned the first time in the Word of God, it follows the same pattern whenever it takes place again, thereby establishing a precedent in the law of God.

Those who truly walk closely with God know that He makes us more and more like Himself, not only in terms of character but also nature. That's right! This is no error. As you walk with the Lord our God, He gives more and more of His omnipotence, omnipresence, and omniscience to us, until we walk in a realm of His own. This is called walking in the Spirit. Such a walk is limited only to the sons of God, concerning whom all of creation is waiting in groaning for the appearance of these saints.

In these last days, God is raising up such a generation of saints who will in fearless and selfless love pursue God as they dance naked before Him before the angry eyes of the world. These shall surely do greater exploits than any recorded in the Bible because the glory of the later house is greater than the glory of the former house!

Such individuals will know that God really means it when He says in His Word that his elect cannot be deceived by even the beast, because they know all things. For as Daniel wrote, a people who know their God shall be strong and do not just exploits but great exploits.

Lady Wisdom builds her house in those who know God and dance naked before God. The benefits of her building her house in you is beyond words in worth (Proverbs 8:14–21).

She says in Proverbs 8:21–31

God imparts to His elect His wisdom Who is the master craftsman by Whom God created everything that exists. This ability to create and determine reality itself is the ultimate gift that God gives to His dancers. It is called dominion. Adam had it and lost it in the garden of Eden when he sinned. But Jesus Christ, the Last Adam, allowed Himself to be butchered naked like a beast and hang accursed on a tree/cross so that He could send the Holy Spirit to restore dominion to His friends who dare to dance naked for Him.

Paul inherited this dominion through the infilling and enveloping presence of the Holy Spirit. He could thus end his prayers by saying word without end. How amazing! Paul knew that he was now one with Wisdom herself in the form of the Holy Spirit, and through his words he was creating a reality that would surely manifest God's purpose in creation. This purpose would continue to expand forever and never end, like the very universe itself! Though a man, by the Spirit, Paul spoke as God Himself.

Most of the church of Jesus Christ today does not understand that this is true spirituality. They have been deluded into thinking that true spirituality is jumping and shouting and speaking in tongues and serving as Pentecostal psychics. This is a strong delusion.

True spirituality is learning how to take back what Adam and Eve lost in the garden of Eden. It is not even the saving of souls, which is a very important part of it. This is spelled out in the gospel that John the Baptist, Jesus Christ, and the early church preached before they were killed off and the message of Jesus Christ subverted by those behind the kingdoms of the world.

The true message of Christ is not conservative but is the most revolutionary one ever spoken. That is why the "officialdom" of His day were in such a hurry to kill Him. The true message is that He and therefore His church or body, by extension, represent the government of Almighty God over all of creation (especially the whole earth), and we are here to establish this government in every sphere of life such as economics, military, society, and religion.

To accomplish this, God the Father has reproduced Himself in the earth, first through Adam and then through Jesus Christ, Who is the Last Adam. The first Adam refused to obey Him because he did not love Him. The Last Adam loved Him enough to live a sinless life and was obedient unto death by the horrible means of flogging, scourging, and crucifixion.

We are supposed to become just like the Last Adam, Who is God the Father in the flesh. Like Christ, we are supposed to live the Word of God until we become the Word made flesh to make this world line up with the perfect will of God the Father. It is only to the extent that Jesus Christ is reproduced in you through intimacy with His Spirit that you will have dominion.

This reproduction is only possible through being born of the Holy Spirit and living a life of radical obedience unto God. This is done by first verbally asking the Holy Spirit in the name of Jesus Christ to take absolute control of us absolutely always. Christ, to this end, instructed us to pray "thy Kingdom come, thy will be done on earth as it is in heaven." To be truly spiritual, we can therefore pray: "thy Kingdom come, thy will be done in my life as it is in heaven." True love for God compels us say to Him in prayer:

"Daddy God, because I love You, give me all that I need to do all that You want me to do each day of my life and to always be just like Your Son Jesus the Christ through the work of Your Spirit in my life."

This is in total contradiction to asking God to do what *you want* Him to do each day. If you begin to pray this way, you will eventually live with all of God manifested in you each day as you dance naked before Him. His will shall become your will when you always live like this. The result of this is that you shall grow into a mature son of God. This is why God says that if you live in Him and His Word lives in you, you can ask for whatever you want, and it shall be given.

Read Galatians 4, use the prayer provided, and live as LORD OF ALL. This is why God created you and therefore true spirituality— the life of defying fallen human logic and obeying Jesus, the lover of our souls. I enjoy jumping and shouting, operating in the gifts of the Spirit, especially prophecy, and dancing in the Spirit more than most. However, after all of this is over, I then put the tremendous power, authority, love, and soundness of mind released by such activities to use, in order to determine and execute the will of God in the earth each day of my life by the grace of God!

Chapter 6

The Heart of the Matter Is Love

1 John 4:7,8

This is because the greatest crisis facing the church of Jesus Christ in the earth today is not defeating Satan or the spiritual forces against which we wrestle (Isaiah 54:14–17).

It is remembering who we are. We are supposed to be the perfect manifestation of love, or God Himself in the earth! When we remember this, we will find that defeating the forces of darkness that are so mightily arrayed against us is par for the course, because they are already defeated (Revelation 20). This is because love never fails.

Because God is love, nothing in the church or creation can work or exist without love. Everything that exists and takes place is in some way a manifestation of the love of God, no matter how horrible things seem to be at times. Ask Job.

All you have to do is humble yourself and ask God for revelation concerning your questions.

Satan cannot defeat the true Christian, because not only was Satan created by God, but he exists by the power of God, as does all else in creation (Colossians 1:15–18).

This is why the planet and creation itself is going increasingly haywire. The church and subsequently the earth itself have stepped outside of God's order. We have done this by living by our fallen intellect instead of praying and fasting and reading the Word of God in worship unto Him until He sends His word for us to perform it by His grace in absolutely every area of our lives.

This is because man shall not live by bread alone but by every word that comes out of the mouth of God! We have become carnal, mixing the sacred with evil. Church boards and pastors hold planning sessions and execute their own agendas in the name of the kingdom of heaven and its Messiah, instead of crying out to Him to control their churches as part of His body by His Spirit.

This is how the early church did it with much success, and there are many examples of this behavior in the Word of God.

The Jerusalem Council only reached a decision when it seemed right to them and to the Holy Spirit, according to the apostle James! Also, Paul was sent out by the Holy Spirit to do not his own ministry but the ministry of the Spirit by him.

He and Silas could not enter Asia, which they thought would be a good field to harvest at that time. Instead they were resisted by the Holy Spirit.

Because there has been a huge increase in rebellion against the laws of God by the people of the world, even the love of most people in the church has become cold, as Paul prophesied that it would in these last days.

Revival will not come to the church and to the earth until the church once again loves God enough to be radically obedient to Him. This will cause many of the faithful to once again be called madmen by the world and by the carnal Christians (Matthew 24:3–31).

This is why the signs and wonders and miracles of God no longer follow most believers, but believers follow them. These signs shall follow them that believe as Christ said, and we therefore do not believe what the early church believed. This is simple deductive reasoning!

We must return to the faith of our fathers who danced naked before God each in his own way.

This is why many well-meaning but misinformed Christians around the world are still waiting for a revival to come that came two thousand years ago!

The apostle Peter himself declared that it had begun in Acts 2:1–21, especially verses 15 to 21:

"Men of Judea and all who dwell in Jerusalem, let this be known to you, and heed my words. For these are not drunk as you suppose, since it is only the third hour of the day (about 9:00 a.m.) But this was spoken by the prophet Joel. And it shall come to pass in the last days says God, That I will pour our my Spirit on all flesh...."

Christians around the world are fully aware that the Holy Spirit was manifested as Peter described many years ago but do not know how to live what was a common experience to the early church. We can pray and fast and even study and quote the Scriptures and go to church every Sunday with little effect seen in our spiritual and physical lives.

This is because obedience is better than sacrifice.

Many Christians today say that they don't even know why they are on the earth! It should be obvious that if Jesus Christ is the Last Adam, then we, as Paul wrote, were born of the Spirit to live as He did (Philippians 1:21).

For me to live is Christ.

This is why Jesus Christ and the early church lived each day of their lives (1 John 3:8, 9): "For this purpose the Son of God was manifested, that He might destroy the works of the devil. Whoever has been born of God does not sin, for His seed remains in Him; and he cannot sin, because he has been born of God."

The worst person that we can fool is ourselves, brethren. Yet many times, we as Christians are guilty of this, so that the people of the world often have more wisdom than we do! This is the sad situation that we find ourselves in, although we say that we have the Spirit of wisdom.

Many of us who are Christians today say terrible words, as mentioned earlier: "Jesus loves me just the way that I am," and we have no intention of changing from our sinful, fallen nature. We also often say that it is impossible for us to not sin. Therefore we call God a liar, as the Scripture above shows. We talk about trying to find ourselves and say "This is who I am; take it or leave it." However, we genuinely expect to one day walk in the power of God, not to mention go to heaven when we die! If you listen now, I am sure you can hear all of hell triumphantly laughing at us.

Can we really expect Jesus to give us His power through which the worlds were formed, to use for our own fallen and fleshly purposes? We would create a mess of unimaginable proportions.

So God in His wisdom is forced to refuse to give His church His power because of our disobedience, and we continue to earnestly pray for it. How long will we go around in this circle? The answer is so clear that it is crystal: until we *change!* (See Romans 12:1–2.)

I beg you therefore, brethren, by the mercies of God, that you present your bodies a living sacrifice, holy and acceptable to God, which is your reasonable service. And do not be conformed to this world, but be transformed by the renewing of your mind, that you may prove what is the good and acceptable and perfect will of God.

God Himself is begging us in His Word to live sinless and holy as Christ lives sinless and holy, by the power of His Spirit, through a life of constant prayer and fasting and meditating on God's Word.

Yet we say that we cannot live like this and ask Him to come to us with His power and might anyway. Are we serious?

Let us repent today. The word *repent* does not mean to feel sorry or guilty in the presence of God, as we often do. It means to *change!*

Ask Jesus Christ to change you by the power of His Spirit into His likeness now and to keep you sinless before the throne of God by His grace. I can assure that the Holy Spirit shall come to you as He did on the day of Pentecost!

Now is the time for global revival. But revival does not come without repentance and holiness or Christlikeness!

Chapter 7

The True Pursuit of Happiness

The word *blessed* means to be happy, fortunate, prosperous, and enviable. The kingdom of heaven consists of righteousness, peace, and joy in the Holy Spirit. As sons and daughters of God, we are therefore all entitled to all these blessings from the Father, because this is how He wants His beloved children to live, according to His covenant with mankind, the Bible.

The problem is that we don't seek Him for the roadmap to our place of blessing, which exists only in His plans for us (Jeremiah 29:11–13). Instead we play for what we see and many times make our own plans. Psalm 35:27 says the life of blessing and prosperity belongs *only* to the servants of God.

The problem is that many Christians don't love God enough to trust Him and become His servants. This is because the life of a servant of God begins when you wake up each morning, and you don't begin to plan for yourself your day's activities, but you ask God what to do. He is supposed to be our day planner and life planner. This is the only way we may walk in the Spirit.

Such a lifestyle requires an amazingly childlike trust in the Father. This why Christ said, that if anyone desires to be the greatest in the kingdom of heaven, he or she must be like a little child. You would expect such a life to be one of bondage. However, it is one of ultimate freedom, for we are constantly rejuvenated by the Spirit, and "where the Spirit of the Lord is there is liberty."

Such liberty cannot be bought, because it is beyond price and cannot be imparted by the laying on of hands, because it is the product of a lifestyle of Davidic worship unto the Father or dancing naked before Him. You must sacrifice and place yourself in bondage unto the Father to truly be free. This is why Paul so delighted in calling himself the bondservant of God. It is the most blessed paradox there is.

This is because bondservants of God walk in the miraculous. We do not follow signs and wonders, but instead signs and wonders follow us. This is because our lives are *always* immersed in the beloved Holy Spirit, who is the source of life itself and life itself.

Try having a love affair with God according to Isaiah 54:5:

"For your Maker is your husband. The Lord of Hosts is His name."

Treat Him as you would treat the perfect lover, for He is the lover of our very souls. Let Him get things moving instead of trying to move them yourself.

Remember that you have an adversary against whom you have no chance in yourself but over whom you are "more than a conqueror in Christ Jesus," our Lord. When you make Christ your *Lord and Master,* you will walk in the "union and communion with God" that we are all baptized into. (See Galatians 3.)

This means that you sit at the right-hand side of God in Christ on His throne, looking down on life. He will therefore lead you to His place of blessing for your life, and you will continuously experience the joy of the Lord, which is our strength.

Trust Him alone, because we often feel frustrated when we are trying to fight a battle which is his—our lives. As David said, "the battle is the Lord's."

In Him is divine provision and blessings that are "far exceedingly and abundantly more than we dare ask for, think of or even dare imagine or dream to be possible" (Ephesians 3:20). For since the Father gave "His only begotten Son" to die on a cross for us in the horrible manner that He did, is there anything good that He would deny us? *Surely not!*

However, our place of blessing is in Him and is therefore a place that was determined by Him even "before He laid the foundations of the earth." To find this place we have to believe in our hearts as David did, that Daddy knows best and act upon this belief because "faith without works is dead." He loves us more than we can imagine and wants only the best for us. This is why in these last days, God is rebuilding the temple of David in the earth (Amos 9:11).

You have sung the songs. Now will you not genuinely ask God to take total control of your life in the name of His Son Jesus the Christ because you love Him and want you and your family to be happy, fortunate, prosperous, enviable, righteous, peaceful, and joyous beyond anything that you can imagine to be possible!

Chapter 8

The Supernatural Life

For the law of the Spirit of the life in Christ Jesus has set us free from the law of sin and death. Romans 8:2

Let us now take a journey deep into the heart of God. You may be wondering why you should take such a journey. You may also wonder what the benefits are of making such a journey. The answers to these questions are really quite mind-blowing!

You will be given access, unlimited authority, power, peace of mind, and financial provision. If you are the suspicious type, you would also know that there must be a catch to this seemingly extravagant claim. Here it is: This journey shall undoubtedly cost you everything. Do you have the courage to make it? By now, you are probably closing this book and wondering what kind of person could ask this of you. His name is Jesus Christ!

Remember, there will be no cowards in heaven!

This is also the first requirement for entry into the kingdom of heaven.

The kingdom of heaven is like a man who heard that there was a treasure hidden in a field and sold all he had to purchase this field and begin to search for this treasure.

Consider for a moment that he sold all that he had to begin the painstaking process of searching for this treasure. This is why so few have really discovered the kingdom of heaven, though most speak of it as though they know it!

This is nothing new. Jesus' Father who sent Him to the earth to preach this gospel had said thousands of years before through the mouth of the prophet Jeremiah that we would only be able to find Him is we seek Him with all our heart.

You see, you cannot enjoy the benefits of the kingdom of heaven without discovering the heart of the king. This is only possible only through extravagantly loving Him by dancing naked before Him. In other words, you have to fall in love with the king to the extent that you then live only for His daily delight as His bride, to have access to His blessings.

He brings His limitless blessings with Himself on only His terms. Yes, our God means it when He says that He is a jealous God, and as unreasonable as it may sometimes seem, nothing in our lives must even begin to compete with our desire for more and more of Him (Colossians 1:16–21).

He is supposed to be our head and is therefore supposed to absolutely *control* us *always!* (John 16:15)

When we love Him this much, He gives all that He is and all that He has, which is everything that exists to us!

When you accept Jesus Christ as your Lord and Savior, you are granted continuously increasing access to all of His authority, power, and financial provision, because you are now one with Him as His bride (Ephesians 1:6–23).

It is often a simple process to accept Jesus Christ as our Savior through His sacrifice for our sins on the cross at Calvary Hill (John 3:16).

However, it is almost impossible to accept Him as our *absolute* Lord, because He will always demand that we worship Him as David did, by dancing naked before His throne. Standing in tremendous opposition to the convert into Christianity is the world and its systems and way of doing things, our own fallen nature, Satan, and worst of all, the carnal or apostate church of Jesus Christ!

This is why God's remnant of dancers in the earth is small and out of the mainstream of church culture. But God is now doing a new thing in the earth. He is preparing a perfect bride for the wedding feast of His Son, the Lamb.

Judgment is therefore now coming to the body of Christ, because we have failed as both salt and light by refusing to dance naked before God. We have become conservative or untrue lovers of God, our husband. She shall soon be trodden under the feet of men (Matthew 5:13, 14).

In order to understand how to walk in love, we must first understand the basis of our covenant with God, which is the basis and substance of life itself.

Chapter 9

An Urgent Call to Repentance

God has set life and death before us and we have chosen
death! (Deuteronomy 30:11–20)

Thousands of years ago, God told His prophet Isaiah that He would
do exactly what He is doing with the weather patterns and the
natural disasters that are taking place with alarming frequency today
(Isaiah 24:5, 6).

"The land and the earth also are defiled by their inhabitants, because
they have transgressed the laws, disregarded the statutes, and broken
the everlasting covenant. Therefore a curse devours the land and the
earth, and they who dwell in it suffer the punishment of their guilt.
Therefore the inhabitants of the land and the earth are scorched
and parched (under the curse of God's wrath), and a few people are
left."

Jesus Himself said in Matthew's gospel, chapter 24, verses 6 to 14,
that there would today be many wars and earthquakes. Long before
that, God said through Moses (Deuteronomy 30:15): "See, I have
set before you this day life and good, death and evil."

These laws were given to man by God in Genesis 9:1–17, Deuteronomy
10:12, 29:9–20. The root of the havoc that is taking place because

of changing weather patterns and natural disasters is not global warming but good old-fashioned sin or the breaking God's laws that He has set in place for His creation, man.

Some would have you believe that this is not the judgment of God that is taking place in the earth today, but here is what He says. Deuteronomy 32:35–43: "Let he who has ears to hear, hear what the Spirit of the Lord is saying to the churches. Return to radical love for God and righteousness. He will no longer tolerate rebellion and false worship in the earth for it is the day of the vengeance of our God! Only those who love Him enough to be His radical lovers and dance naked before Him will be spared the wrath that has begun."

Isaiah 61:1, 2

Unconvinced? Well, consider the global warming argument that is so stupid that it will not be given much space in this book. Could global warming cause the tsunamis and earthquakes that the earth has been experiencing with increasing frequency recently?

That was a purely rhetorical question. Is global warming causing the snowstorms that are wreaking chaos in North America and Europe? Could it have caused a volcano in Iceland to erupt and shut down air traffic in Europe recently? The answer is so obvious, it is appalling. No!

The solution: Ask God to teach you how to love Him enough that you will always keep His laws, not because you are afraid of Him destroying you and your family, but because you want to keep them. Also ask Him for the courage to be radically obedient to Him by defying your fallen logic each day and crucifying your flesh as you dance naked in Him!

Will you not accept Jesus Christ as your Lord and God?

If you do so, His Spirit will come into you, and you can ask Him to change your heart as the ancient prophets foretold.

Many, many, many people will perish in the earth in the years ahead for breaking the laws of God, even if they do not believe so (Psalm 110:5–7), but you do not have to be one of them! Abraham, the father of our faith, established an important principle in Genesis 18:23–25. This is that God, being a just or good judge, cannot judge the righteous with the wicked.

The word *righteous* means to be in right standing with God. This means that if you ask Him to teach you how to *always* do, say, and think what He wants you to as well as to *always* be who He wants you to be through the Holy Spirit writing His laws upon your heart, you will not die in His judgments that are now striking the earth.

Today life and good, death and evil have been set before you.
I humble myself, and I now beg you to choose life!

Chapter 10

The Coming Massive Spiritual and Physical Attack upon the Church of Jesus Christ

Blow the trumpet in Zion …Joel 2: 1-27

A terrible army is advancing against the saints of God. Those who are tuned in to what is taking place in the supernatural alone know of its determined march. Many who swore their lives to the Lamb of God will flee before it in terror because they do not truly know their God. The most interesting thing about this army is that God says that it is His army. This is because it is His act of righteous judgment on His own church in the earth.

We can see their ranks in the courts, the media, the arts and entertainment, the corruption of the economic systems, and in virtually every sphere of life. When what the Word of God calls the occult or gross darkness started to become mainstream culture, I started to get very nervous. So I cried out to God, asking Him for the meaning of this advance of the kingdom of darkness. That which previously hid itself was now becoming the norm.

The answer I received stunned me. Deep within my spirit, I one day heard the Lord say, "Satan is mobilizing his army." I was instructed by the Spirit of the Lord to let Him lead me through the Scriptures and show me where it is mentioned, its divine purpose, and its fate (Daniel 7:25).

In the shadows is its general, the beast, who has already been allowed by the Father to put in motion the events that would thrust him to world leadership. There are only three peoples in his way. They are the true church of Jesus Christ, the nation of Israel, and the United States of America and her mighty army.

Even in her weakened state, the beast knows that God's remnant in the earth is his greatest adversary. This is because what we accept on earth is accepted in heaven, and whatever we reject on earth is rejected in heaven. Heaven, led by her champion, the King of Kings and Lord of Lords, then executes these positions through His ambassadors in the earth. So if there is only one true believer in the earth, the beast cannot be revealed but has to continue to act from the shadows. Therefore, he and his globalists of the new world order will soon return martyrdom to the western nations.

Israel is hated by him and his master Satan more than any nation in the earth, even though the Scriptures tell us that he is a Jew. His forerunner, Adolph Hitler, the chancellor of Nazi Germany, killed nearly 6 million Jews because of God's covenant with Abraham's seed. The Bible also tells us that they will soon discover the massive oil reserves for which they are now searching in the territory of Asher (Deuteronomy 33:24). Together with her industrial, technological, and agricultural growth, Israel is now becoming a praise in the earth unto our God as He said she would. We therefore stand on the verge of the battle of Gog and Magog and the global earthquake that will give victory to Israel.

The beast will send an army against the United States, I believe soon. This invading force will be defeated. President Benyamin Netanyahu has been raised up by God to lead His people during this coming time of war and crisis, and I believe that he is spoken of by the prophet Jeremiah and will destroy the armies that come against Israel in these last days (Jeremiah 30:18–24).

The United States of America is squarely in the beast's crosshairs because she was raised up by God to stop the rise of the new world order that is coming not out of Europe but Eurasia. He is therefore called the Assyrian in the book of Isaiah. He does not have to be the evil genius to know that America's alliance with Britain during World War Two was a shadow of things to come. He cannot prevent it from taking place again during the upcoming global conflict so he must attempt to destroy both the lion (America) and the eagle (Britain)!

I am not a conspiracy theorist. These things must come to pass for Scripture to be fulfilled. What is most interesting is that the Bible says that they are in our best interest. God is going to become the true Lord of His church. Those who rely on human reason or a combination of human reason and divine leadership will fail miserably in these days. It is the time of the true prophets, priests, and kings of God to reign in the earth.

The pains that are about to come upon the church are the birth pains of Messiah. They will birth Christ in His resurrection power, the powers of the age to come, and the wisdom of the ages in His church. This is when we shall see the knowledge of the glory of God cover the earth as the waters cover the sea. The wealth of the wicked will not just wake up one morning and decide to walk into the church. It shall and must be won!

Micah 4:11–13

Joel 3:9–11, 18–21

It is a time for warfare in the earth, and the church of Jesus Christ is for the most part ignoring the trumpet that has sounded in heaven for her to mobilize. Ministers of the gospel are fighting turf wars among themselves, instead of embracing each other in genuine brotherly love. There is a saying that the greatest loyalty among men is developed in the trenches on the battlefield. This is coming today to the church. Jesus Christ's prayer to the Father for unity in His bride will be answered positively by Him (John 17:6–19).

Surely Malachi 2:8 has come to pass. This is why! We have, as a church, entered into Malachi 1:6–14 by refusing to symbolically dance naked before God.

You may say that this Scripture speaks to Israel, but have we done any differently? We have, for the most part, refused to give God the absolute obedience to His Spirit that He demands, as Malachi 3:13–18 said we would! God is only now starting to pour out His wrath on the earth as the rebellion of Psalm 2:1–3 takes place and the great confederacy against Israel of Psalm 83 is being formed. However, as Malachi wrote, God will tremendously bless the remnant that He has kept for Himself in the earth during these times.

Are you a part of that remnant? Do you symbolically dance naked before God, to be spared the wrath that is unfolding as you read this book?

Chapter 11

The Old and the New Weapons of Our Warfare Straight from the Armory of Heaven

The Lord has opened His armory, And has brought out the weapons of His indignation; For this is the work of the Lord God of hosts ... (Jeremiah 50:25)

God's entire quest since the fall of man has been to get back what He had with man in the garden of Eden. This is intimacy, at an even greater intensity. The biblical principle that He has established in His Word is that the glory of the latter house is greater than the glory of the former house!

You may wonder what this has to do with the weapons of our warfare.

It is my word to you that unless you have intimacy with God, you have no access to the armory of God, and you will therefore have no spiritual weapons. Those who rely on hype, charisma, and manipulation and political finesse in the church will be publicly humiliated in this age. Their lack of armor will be painfully exposed for all the world to see. This has already begun in the glare of the international media.

The true armor of God is the manifested as the supernatural presence of God Himself in your life and around your physical body. It is not theoretical or imagined. The reason most of the church today is doing such a poor job at spiritual warfare is because they have very little or no armor, so they are being ruled by the enemy. In other words, Satan strikes them on a regular basis, and they ignore what is taking place.

But others see and laugh at us! (For more information on the condition of the state of the armor of God being worn by most Christians today, read *The Quest, The Call,* and *A Prophetic Vision of the 21st Century* by Rick Joyner. These are the only books by this author that I have proven to be truth in my own experience, and I can therefore now endorse them and no others by him in this book.)

The armor of God is a living, breathing thing. It is the manifestation of the attributes and presence of Christ Himself clothing the believer. How? The answer is quite simple. The helmet is salvation, which is the process of becoming like Christ. It is taken from the root word *salvage*.

Accepting Jesus Christ as your Lord and Savior is only the start of this process in which we are supposed to progressively live more and more as Christ lived (Philippians 2:12–15) and ultimately be just as He is today (1John 4:17b) in the world.

Christ is the physical manifestation of the Father. The Father is Spirit; when the Father comes down to the earth to act in the physical to bring justice, He Himself has to put on the armor of God, His physical abilities. This is because Christ is His physical self, to act in the natural. Read Isaiah 59:16–21.

So the armor of God has always existed. It was not discovered by Paul in the book of Ephesians chapter 6, verses 10 to 18.

It has existed as long as the physical world has existed and is what we need to wear to be effective in the earth, just as the Father Himself does. So let's take a closer look at it.

The breastplate is righteousness, and our righteousness is in being just like Jesus Christ in every way. The word *righteousness* means to be in right standing with God, as said earlier. It literally means to absolutely always be doing, saying, thinking, and being who and what the Father wants us to be, as Christ did and does to this day (John 5:19, 20).

I hope that you are getting nervous by now, because you would have realized that this state is impossible to us in ourselves. Yet Jesus clearly did it, and we are clearly expected to do the same! How did He do this? Turn to Isaiah 11:2–6.

For everything that you need to do, say, think, or be, there is a manifestation of the Spirit of God. Jesus Christ understood this. He first submitted Himself to the Holy Spirit as a conscious covenant or agreement with God the Father and carried it out with a life of prayer and fasting and a perfect knowledge of the Word of God.

This level of submission is one that you can *only* get to by admitting to God that you cannot do it yourself, and you desperately need Him to do it by His crucifying your flesh each day. This process will hurt, and the closer you come to the point where each day it is not you who lives but Christ who lives in you, the more it will hurt. You will therefore have to ask God to tie you to His altar like an ancient sacrificial animal was!

The Bible promises you this when it says that the life of an individual is full of trouble (Job 14:1). The challenge is to let the trouble kill your fallen nature, so that you can have the resurrection power of Christ, and then nothing will be impossible to you. The only way that you can have the resurrection power of God that raised Christ from the dead and gave Him His new resurrection body is by sharing in His suffering (Philippians 3:1–11).

If you do this correctly, you will come through your trouble and really be more than a conqueror! It will not just be a popular slogan or form of hype. This is called falling forward.

The girdle of the armor is truth, and Christ is the Truth or the Living Word. Knowledge of the *logos* (the written Word of God) alone will not be enough. You *must* ask God for a revelation of the true meaning of His Word or you are wasting your time reading it!

You must therefore always ask God to reveal His mysteries to you as kings in Christ (Proverbs 25:2).

Our feet are also shod with the gospel of peace, and Jesus Christ is the Prince of Peace. We are to therefore put on the very peace-loving nature of Christ in whom the fullness of the Godhead rests. This is our spiritual protection. The only way we can walk securely with the Father is to adopt the nature of the Son through the work of the Spirit in our lives. This therefore covers our feet.

It follows that the only way we can adopt the nature of the Son is by becoming progressively more intimate with the Spirit of God or God Himself in our everyday lives.

Finally, the shield is the shield of faith. Faith is really the knowledge of God that He has of Himself! So we do not have to recite a litany about putting on the armor of God each day of our lives. This is stupid and empty religion!

Embrace the Father through submitting yourself absolutely to the work of the Holy Spirit each moment of each day of your life, and you will learn to walk just as Christ does now. (See 1 John 4:17b.)

This is the *true* armor of God, and it is our *only* protection in spiritual warfare, which we *cannot* avoid in this life. It has been said that those who don't spend much time in prayer are easy prey for Satan.

We can only ignore this truth to our own destruction. If you do not fight against the forces of darkness each day, they will steal from you, take life from you, and ultimately destroy you! This is their purpose:

to make you into a person of war, even as God is a person of war. One of His most frequently used names in the Bible is the Lord of Hosts or the God who commands the armies of heaven!

REMEMBER that you have not because you ask not!

Ask God to teach you how to have a perfect

spiritual armor using this word from God as a starting point!

The greatest spiritual weapon of all is now being given to the church of Jesus Christ. It is the scepter of God or His rod of iron with which He will judge and rule the nations of the earth (Psalm 2:9 and Psalm 110:3).

Up till this time, the church has followed the pattern of Queen Esther in spiritual warfare. We have prayed and fasted and approached the King to stretch forth His scepter toward us and give judgment in our favor. This is immaturity and is not what Christ died for!

It is now time for a new breed of believers who daily dance naked before God to wield the scepter of God themselves and reign as kings in the earth. It is the scepter of the righteous and righteousness.

Thus, the extent to which a believer shall wield the scepter of God will be determined by his level of righteousness and obedience to the Father (Hebrews 1:8b). We have already looked at the example of Christ, but it is important to note that even the Holy Spirit submits Himself absolutely to the will of the Father. He only says what He hears the Father saying.

The new covenant in Christ Jesus is therefore one of always abandoning oneself absolutely to the control of the Father through the work of the Holy Spirit in our lives. No carnal Christian will ever have access to the authority and power available to those spiritual believers who wield the scepter of God. The Father will not tolerate iniquity in His kingdom (Psalm 103:19). And He will now purge the church to prepare a bride for His Son.

Divine holiness, righteousness, perfection, and obedience are therefore vital to believers receiving the anointing and then appointment as kings in the earth (Hebrews 2:8).

The process the believer will have to go through to wield this scepter will not be an easy one, and that is an understatement. The heart of each saint will be the deciding factor. Most, like Israel in the wilderness, will err in their hearts (Hebrews 3:10, 11). They will not love God enough to dance naked before Him.

The appointment as kings and lords of all is the believer's promised land in the earth. A young generation will rise up to take the mantle of leadership in the church. In a time of massive social, economic, and political upheaval in the earth, they will take the gospel of the kingdom of heaven back to the streets. Like David, they will each have a heart after God's own heart and will work in tandem with those of the previous generation who, like Samuel, have the very heart of God. This is God's own dynamic duo or one-two combination.

They will be a company of saints with faith never seen before in the earth, because faith works by love, and they will lay down their lives in love for God. This is unlike other Christians who, like Israel in the wilderness did, treat God like an ATM that could never satisfy their desires (Hebrews 3:15b–19).

Their living faith will produce an unprecedented era of signs, wonders, and miracles in the earth as they wield the scepter of God. They will not only embrace the true meaning of the cross but will enjoy doing so.

This company of saints will each have the limitless fullness of the anointing of God, even as Christ has it. They will thus do greater works than He did. They will be carriers of the very glory of God Himself, His *shekinah* glory. They will be the true temples of God and represent the ark of the covenant in the earth, even as Christ is the ark. They will be flaming ministers of God and will light the earth, even as fire from heaven lit God's temple in ancient times.

They will put on the zeal of the Lord and wear it as a cloak, even as the Father does. Their love and passion for Jesus will shock and discomfit many in the church, but it will make them able to do great exploits that previous generations could not even dream of.

In the time of spiritual darkness that has begun in the earth, many believers will come under the attack of witchcraft (Isaiah 60).

God will place a ring of fire around the dwelling places of the elect, even as He has around Israel.

He will be the teacher and mentor of his elect (Isaiah 54:13), and their wisdom, knowledge, understanding, and insight will stun the world. They will use the key of knowledge of the ancient prophets to truly know all things (Luke 11:52). Many will understand how to miraculously know the Holy Spirit as their constant comforter or helper, advisor, intercessor, advocate/ lawyer before the throne of God, strengthener and as one on standby to give them victory in this life.

Christians will once again be pilgrims in the earth … with no love for this life. We will live each day as martyrs under the power of the blood of Christ. The word of our testimony will be the witness of the Lordship of Jesus Christ in the affairs of men. Our words will truly be spirit and life.

God will entrust us with the sword of the Spirit which is His word and we will rule the earth. Isaiah 59:21. In dangerous times God will cover us with His wings even as a hen covers her chicks.

We will have the mantle of kings because they will live as servants. "For the Son of man come into the earth not to be served but to serve." Such servant leaders will wash the feet of the faithful as Christ did. Not literally, but they will be so intimate and in love with their charges that they will allow themselves to be considered corrupt in the eyes of the religious crowd. To reign in God's kingdom is to serve, and to serve is to reign! (Matthew 20:25–28)

Chapter 12

Shaping Reality 101

The movie series of *The Matrix* has produced three stunning blockbusters. What is surprising about this is that at the core of the movie is the questioning about the very nature of reality. The popularity of such a searching critique of life— that reality is not in fact real—is surprising for Western civilization. Of course, with all the action, you can forget the critique and just watch Neo kill agents.

This is because at some point in time, we must each sit back and question the very nature of reality ourselves, because this determines the very way in which we live our lives. I have staked my life on the Bible being the true and infallible Word of God, and this has strengthened me immeasurably, because it has allowed God to continuously strengthen me in my inner man, which is where it counts the most. This is how I dance naked before God.

The Bible clearly states that the basic nature of the reality in which we live is spiritual and that the spiritual determines everything else. That is "in the beginning, God." The Father is quite clearly a Spirit, and they that worship Him must first worship Him in Spirit and then in truth. Creation began in the spiritual realm and will one day end from it when a new heaven and earth are created.

We worship God in Spirit by "walking in the Spirit" and not in the flesh. For too long, the bride of Christ has viewed worship as something to do on a Sunday morning for one hour and not as a lifestyle or way of life (for practice twenty-four hours a day, seven days a week). If you truly desire to master the Christian experience, you must ask the Father to teach you how to "walk in the Spirit."

"For as many as are led by the Spirit of God these are the sons of God" (Romans 8:12–17).

Seek this rich spiritual life, and you will find that the rewards are immeasurable. The Father Himself fills you with power in your daily experience on a perpetual basis. He is a limitless source of power because, as David said, "power belongeth to God." Power to be happy, fortunate, prosperous, and enviable, as the word *blessed* means, is yours for the taking in the Spirit life.

Also, no man knows a man but the spirit of a man, and likewise no one knows God as deeply as His own Spirit. This is why Christ had to die and the Holy Spirit had to come to the earth, because no one knows the Father like He does, for He is His very essence. Seek a deep and personal relationship with Him through our mediator, the Lord Jesus Christ, and you will know God like very few ever have.

This is because most persons get caught up in externalities and do not seek the heart of the Father as David did. Seek the heart of God. God, seated upon the throne of Grace in heaven one day, heard a scrawny little Hebrew boy worshiping Him in spirit and in truth and took that boy from the hillside to the throne of Israel, making him one of the greatest kings Israel and the world ever had.

GOD WILL DO ABSOLUTELY ANYTHING FOR THE GOOD OF A TRUE WORSHIPER OF HIM!

God owns the earth. He made man its caretaker or steward. At no time did He give ownership of the earth to man (Psalm 24:1, 2).

He controls the very fate of each person in human history, no matter what that person may or may not believe (Proverbs 16:9).

The Lord even controls the hearts of men (Proverbs 21:1).

Man was not created to act according to his own will but God's, as Ephesians 2:10 clearly states!

That's all for now, folks! I always wanted to say that.